THIS SAILING

LOG BOOK

BELONGS TO:

DATE: _____

PLACE: _____

WEATHER:

MY NOTES:

_____

_____

_____

_____

_____

HOW I FEEL ABOUT MY SAILING TODAY

A RECORD OF MY DAY:

DATE: _____

PLACE: _____

WEATHER:

MY NOTES:

_____

_____

_____

_____

_____

HOW I FEEL ABOUT MY SAILING TODAY

A RECORD OF MY DAY:

DATE: _____

PLACE: _____

WEATHER:

MY NOTES:

_____
_____
_____
_____
_____

HOW I FEEL ABOUT MY SAILING TODAY

A RECORD OF MY DAY:

DATE: _____

PLACE: _____

WEATHER:

MY NOTES:

_____
_____
_____
_____
_____

HOW I FEEL ABOUT MY SAILING TODAY

A RECORD OF MY DAY:

DATE: _____

PLACE: _____

WEATHER:

MY NOTES:

_____

_____

_____

_____

_____

HOW I FEEL ABOUT MY SAILING TODAY

A RECORD OF MY DAY:

DATE: _____

PLACE: _____

WEATHER:

MY NOTES:

_____
_____
_____
_____
_____

HOW I FEEL ABOUT MY SAILING TODAY

A RECORD OF MY DAY:

DATE: _____

PLACE: _____

WEATHER:

MY NOTES:

_____

_____

_____

_____

_____

HOW I FEEL ABOUT MY SAILING TODAY

A RECORD OF MY DAY:

DATE: _____

PLACE: _____

WEATHER:

MY NOTES:

_____

_____

_____

_____

_____

HOW I FEEL ABOUT MY SAILING TODAY

A RECORD OF MY DAY:

DATE: _____

PLACE: _____

WEATHER:

MY NOTES:

_____

_____

_____

_____

_____

HOW I FEEL ABOUT MY SAILING TODAY

A RECORD OF MY DAY:

```
```

DATE: _____

PLACE: _____

WEATHER:

MY NOTES:

_____

_____

_____

_____

_____

HOW I FEEL ABOUT MY SAILING TODAY

A RECORD OF MY DAY:

DATE: _____

PLACE: _____

WEATHER:

MY NOTES:

_____

_____

_____

_____

_____

HOW I FEEL ABOUT MY SAILING TODAY

A RECORD OF MY DAY:

DATE: _____

PLACE: _____

WEATHER:

MY NOTES:

_____

_____

_____

_____

_____

HOW I FEEL ABOUT MY SAILING TODAY

A RECORD OF MY DAY:

DATE: _____

PLACE: _____

WEATHER:

MY NOTES:

_____

_____

_____

_____

_____

HOW I FEEL ABOUT MY SAILING TODAY

A RECORD OF MY DAY:

DATE: _____

PLACE: _____

WEATHER:

MY NOTES:

_____
_____
_____
_____
_____

HOW I FEEL ABOUT MY SAILING TODAY

A RECORD OF MY DAY:

DATE: _____

PLACE: _____

WEATHER:

MY NOTES:

_____
_____
_____
_____
_____

HOW I FEEL ABOUT MY SAILING TODAY

A RECORD OF MY DAY:

DATE: _____

PLACE: _____

WEATHER:

MY NOTES:

_____

_____

_____

_____

_____

HOW I FEEL ABOUT MY SAILING TODAY

A RECORD OF MY DAY:

DATE: _____

PLACE: _____

WEATHER:

MY NOTES:

_____

_____

_____

_____

_____

HOW I FEEL ABOUT MY SAILING TODAY

A RECORD OF MY DAY:

DATE: _____

PLACE: _____

WEATHER:

MY NOTES:

_____

_____

_____

_____

_____

HOW I FEEL ABOUT MY SAILING TODAY

A RECORD OF MY DAY:

DATE: _____

PLACE: _____

WEATHER:

MY NOTES:

_____
_____
_____
_____
_____

HOW I FEEL ABOUT MY SAILING TODAY

A RECORD OF MY DAY:

DATE: _____

PLACE: _____

WEATHER:

MY NOTES:

_____

_____

_____

_____

_____

HOW I FEEL ABOUT MY SAILING TODAY

A RECORD OF MY DAY:

DATE: _____

PLACE: _____

WEATHER:

MY NOTES:

_____
_____
_____
_____
_____

HOW I FEEL ABOUT MY SAILING TODAY

A RECORD OF MY DAY:

DATE: _____

PLACE: _____

WEATHER:

MY NOTES:

_____

_____

_____

_____

_____

HOW I FEEL ABOUT MY SAILING TODAY

A RECORD OF MY DAY:

DATE: _____

PLACE: _____

WEATHER:

MY NOTES:

_____

_____

_____

_____

_____

HOW I FEEL ABOUT MY SAILING TODAY

A RECORD OF MY DAY:

DATE: _____

PLACE: _____

WEATHER:

MY NOTES:

_____
_____
_____
_____
_____
_____

HOW I FEEL ABOUT MY SAILING TODAY

A RECORD OF MY DAY:

DATE: _____

PLACE: _____

WEATHER:

MY NOTES:

_____
_____
_____
_____
_____

HOW I FEEL ABOUT MY SAILING TODAY

A RECORD OF MY DAY:

DATE: _____

PLACE: _____

WEATHER:

MY NOTES:

_____

_____

_____

_____

_____

HOW I FEEL ABOUT MY SAILING TODAY

A RECORD OF MY DAY:

DATE: _____

PLACE: _____

WEATHER:

MY NOTES:

_____

_____

_____

_____

_____

HOW I FEEL ABOUT MY SAILING TODAY

A RECORD OF MY DAY:

DATE: _____

PLACE: _____

WEATHER:

MY NOTES:

_____

_____

_____

_____

_____

HOW I FEEL ABOUT MY SAILING TODAY

A RECORD OF MY DAY:

DATE: _____

PLACE: _____

WEATHER:

MY NOTES:

_____
_____
_____
_____
_____

HOW I FEEL ABOUT MY SAILING TODAY

A RECORD OF MY DAY:

DATE: _____

PLACE: _____

WEATHER:

MY NOTES:

_____

_____

_____

_____

_____

HOW I FEEL ABOUT MY SAILING TODAY

A RECORD OF MY DAY:

DATE: _____

PLACE: _____

WEATHER:

MY NOTES:

_____

_____

_____

_____

_____

HOW I FEEL ABOUT MY SAILING TODAY

A RECORD OF MY DAY:

DATE: _____

PLACE: _____

WEATHER:

MY NOTES:

_____

_____

_____

_____

_____

HOW I FEEL ABOUT MY SAILING TODAY

A RECORD OF MY DAY:

DATE: _____

PLACE: _____

WEATHER:

MY NOTES:

_____

_____

_____

_____

_____

HOW I FEEL ABOUT MY SAILING TODAY

A RECORD OF MY DAY:

DATE: _____

PLACE: _____

WEATHER:

MY NOTES:

_____

_____

_____

_____

_____

HOW I FEEL ABOUT MY SAILING TODAY

A RECORD OF MY DAY:

DATE: _____

PLACE: _____

WEATHER:

MY NOTES:

_____

_____

_____

_____

_____

HOW I FEEL ABOUT MY SAILING TODAY

A RECORD OF MY DAY:

DATE: _____

PLACE: _____

WEATHER:

MY NOTES:

_____
_____
_____
_____
_____
_____

HOW I FEEL ABOUT MY SAILING TODAY

A RECORD OF MY DAY:

DATE: _____

PLACE: _____

WEATHER:

MY NOTES:

_____

_____

_____

_____

_____

HOW I FEEL ABOUT MY SAILING TODAY

A RECORD OF MY DAY:

DATE: _____

PLACE: _____

WEATHER:

MY NOTES:

_____

_____

_____

_____

_____

HOW I FEEL ABOUT MY SAILING TODAY

A RECORD OF MY DAY:

DATE: _____

PLACE: _____

WEATHER:

MY NOTES:
_____
_____
_____
_____
_____

HOW I FEEL ABOUT MY SAILING TODAY

A RECORD OF MY DAY:

DATE: _____

PLACE: _____

WEATHER:

MY NOTES:

_____
_____
_____
_____
_____

HOW I FEEL ABOUT MY SAILING TODAY

A RECORD OF MY DAY:

DATE: _____

PLACE: _____

WEATHER:

MY NOTES:

_____
_____
_____
_____
_____

HOW I FEEL ABOUT MY SAILING TODAY

A RECORD OF MY DAY:

DATE: _____

PLACE: _____

WEATHER:

MY NOTES:

_____
_____
_____
_____
_____

HOW I FEEL ABOUT MY SAILING TODAY

A RECORD OF MY DAY:

DATE: _____

PLACE: _____

WEATHER:

MY NOTES:

_____
_____
_____
_____
_____

HOW I FEEL ABOUT MY SAILING TODAY

A RECORD OF MY DAY:

DATE: _____

PLACE: _____

WEATHER:

MY NOTES:

_____
_____
_____
_____
_____

HOW I FEEL ABOUT MY SAILING TODAY

A RECORD OF MY DAY:

DATE: _____

PLACE: _____

WEATHER:

MY NOTES:

_____

_____

_____

_____

_____

HOW I FEEL ABOUT MY SAILING TODAY

A RECORD OF MY DAY:

DATE: _____

PLACE: _____

WEATHER:

MY NOTES:

_____

_____

_____

_____

_____

HOW I FEEL ABOUT MY SAILING TODAY

A RECORD OF MY DAY:

DATE: _____

PLACE: _____

WEATHER:

MY NOTES:

_____

_____

_____

_____

_____

HOW I FEEL ABOUT MY SAILING TODAY

A RECORD OF MY DAY:

DATE: _____

PLACE: _____

WEATHER:

MY NOTES:

_____
_____
_____
_____
_____
_____

HOW I FEEL ABOUT MY SAILING TODAY

A RECORD OF MY DAY:

DATE: _____

PLACE: _____

WEATHER:

MY NOTES:

_____
_____
_____
_____
_____

HOW I FEEL ABOUT MY SAILING TODAY

A RECORD OF MY DAY:

DATE: _____

PLACE: _____

WEATHER:

MY NOTES:

_____

_____

_____

_____

_____

HOW I FEEL ABOUT MY SAILING TODAY

A RECORD OF MY DAY:

DATE: _____

PLACE: _____

WEATHER:

MY NOTES:
_____
_____
_____
_____
_____

HOW I FEEL ABOUT MY SAILING TODAY

A RECORD OF MY DAY:

DATE: _____

PLACE: _____

WEATHER:

MY NOTES:

_____
_____
_____
_____
_____

HOW I FEEL ABOUT MY SAILING TODAY

A RECORD OF MY DAY:

DATE: _____

PLACE: _____

WEATHER:

MY NOTES:

_____

_____

_____

_____

_____

HOW I FEEL ABOUT MY SAILING TODAY

A RECORD OF MY DAY:

DATE: _____

PLACE: _____

WEATHER:

MY NOTES:

_____
_____
_____
_____
_____
_____

HOW I FEEL ABOUT MY SAILING TODAY

A RECORD OF MY DAY:

DATE: _____

PLACE: _____

WEATHER:

MY NOTES:

_____

_____

_____

_____

_____

HOW I FEEL ABOUT MY SAILING TODAY

A RECORD OF MY DAY:

DATE: _____

PLACE: _____

WEATHER:

MY NOTES:

_____
_____
_____
_____
_____

HOW I FEEL ABOUT MY SAILING TODAY

A RECORD OF MY DAY:

DATE: _____

PLACE: _____

WEATHER:

MY NOTES:

_____

_____

_____

_____

_____

HOW I FEEL ABOUT MY SAILING TODAY

A RECORD OF MY DAY:

DATE: _____

PLACE: _____

WEATHER:

MY NOTES:

_____
_____
_____
_____
_____

HOW I FEEL ABOUT MY SAILING TODAY

A RECORD OF MY DAY:

DATE: _____

PLACE: _____

WEATHER:

MY NOTES:

_____

_____

_____

_____

_____

HOW I FEEL ABOUT MY SAILING TODAY

A RECORD OF MY DAY:

DATE: _____

PLACE: _____

WEATHER:

MY NOTES:

_____
_____
_____
_____
_____
_____

HOW I FEEL ABOUT MY SAILING TODAY

A RECORD OF MY DAY:

DATE: _____

PLACE: _____

WEATHER:

MY NOTES:

_____

_____

_____

_____

_____

HOW I FEEL ABOUT MY SAILING TODAY

A RECORD OF MY DAY:

DATE: _____

PLACE: _____

WEATHER:

MY NOTES:

_____

_____

_____

_____

_____

HOW I FEEL ABOUT MY SAILING TODAY

A RECORD OF MY DAY:

DATE: _____

PLACE: _____

WEATHER:

MY NOTES:

_____

_____

_____

_____

_____

HOW I FEEL ABOUT MY SAILING TODAY

A RECORD OF MY DAY:

DATE: _____

PLACE: _____

WEATHER:

MY NOTES:

_____

_____

_____

_____

_____

HOW I FEEL ABOUT MY SAILING TODAY

A RECORD OF MY DAY:

DATE: _____

PLACE: _____

WEATHER:

MY NOTES:

_____

_____

_____

_____

_____

HOW I FEEL ABOUT MY SAILING TODAY

A RECORD OF MY DAY:

DATE: _____

PLACE: _____

WEATHER:

MY NOTES:

_____
_____
_____
_____
_____
_____

HOW I FEEL ABOUT MY SAILING TODAY

A RECORD OF MY DAY:

DATE: _____

PLACE: _____

WEATHER:

MY NOTES:

_____

_____

_____

_____

_____

HOW I FEEL ABOUT MY SAILING TODAY

A RECORD OF MY DAY:

DATE: _____

PLACE: _____

WEATHER:

MY NOTES:

_____
_____
_____
_____
_____

HOW I FEEL ABOUT MY SAILING TODAY

A RECORD OF MY DAY:

DATE: _____

PLACE: _____

WEATHER:

MY NOTES:

_____

_____

_____

_____

_____

HOW I FEEL ABOUT MY SAILING TODAY

A RECORD OF MY DAY:

DATE: _____

PLACE: _____

WEATHER:

MY NOTES:

_____

_____

_____

_____

_____

HOW I FEEL ABOUT MY SAILING TODAY

A RECORD OF MY DAY:

DATE: _____

PLACE: _____

WEATHER:

MY NOTES:

_____
_____
_____
_____
_____

HOW I FEEL ABOUT MY SAILING TODAY

A RECORD OF MY DAY:

DATE: _____

PLACE: _____

WEATHER:

MY NOTES:

_____

_____

_____

_____

_____

_____

HOW I FEEL ABOUT MY SAILING TODAY

A RECORD OF MY DAY:

DATE: _____

PLACE: _____

WEATHER:

MY NOTES:

_____

_____

_____

_____

_____

HOW I FEEL ABOUT MY SAILING TODAY

A RECORD OF MY DAY:

DATE: _____

PLACE: _____

WEATHER:

MY NOTES:

_____

_____

_____

_____

_____

HOW I FEEL ABOUT MY SAILING TODAY

A RECORD OF MY DAY:

DATE: _____

PLACE: _____

WEATHER:

MY NOTES:

_____

_____

_____

_____

_____

HOW I FEEL ABOUT MY SAILING TODAY

A RECORD OF MY DAY:

DATE: _____

PLACE: _____

WEATHER:

MY NOTES:

_____

_____

_____

_____

_____

HOW I FEEL ABOUT MY SAILING TODAY

A RECORD OF MY DAY:

DATE: _____

PLACE: _____

WEATHER:

MY NOTES:

_____

_____

_____

_____

_____

HOW I FEEL ABOUT MY SAILING TODAY

A RECORD OF MY DAY:

DATE: _____

PLACE: _____

WEATHER:

MY NOTES:

_____

_____

_____

_____

_____

_____

HOW I FEEL ABOUT MY SAILING TODAY

A RECORD OF MY DAY:

```



```

DATE: _____

PLACE: _____

WEATHER:

MY NOTES:

_____

_____

_____

_____

_____

HOW I FEEL ABOUT MY SAILING TODAY

A RECORD OF MY DAY:

DATE: _____

PLACE: _____

WEATHER:

MY NOTES:

_____

_____

_____

_____

_____

HOW I FEEL ABOUT MY SAILING TODAY

A RECORD OF MY DAY:

DATE: _____

PLACE: _____

WEATHER:

MY NOTES:

_____

_____

_____

_____

_____

HOW I FEEL ABOUT MY SAILING TODAY

A RECORD OF MY DAY:

DATE: _____

PLACE: _____

WEATHER:

MY NOTES:

_____

_____

_____

_____

_____

HOW I FEEL ABOUT MY SAILING TODAY

A RECORD OF MY DAY:

DATE: _____

PLACE: _____

WEATHER:

MY NOTES:

_____

_____

_____

_____

_____

HOW I FEEL ABOUT MY SAILING TODAY

A RECORD OF MY DAY:

DATE: _____

PLACE: _____

WEATHER:

MY NOTES:

_____
_____
_____
_____
_____
_____

HOW I FEEL ABOUT MY SAILING TODAY

A RECORD OF MY DAY:

DATE: _____

PLACE: _____

WEATHER:

MY NOTES:

_____
_____
_____
_____
_____

HOW I FEEL ABOUT MY SAILING TODAY

A RECORD OF MY DAY:

DATE: _____

PLACE: _____

WEATHER:

MY NOTES:

_____
_____
_____
_____
_____

HOW I FEEL ABOUT MY SAILING TODAY

A RECORD OF MY DAY:

DATE: _____

PLACE: _____

WEATHER:

MY NOTES:

_____

_____

_____

_____

_____

HOW I FEEL ABOUT MY SAILING TODAY

A RECORD OF MY DAY:

DATE: _____

PLACE: _____

WEATHER:

MY NOTES:

_____
_____
_____
_____
_____

HOW I FEEL ABOUT MY SAILING TODAY

A RECORD OF MY DAY:

DATE: _____

PLACE: _____

WEATHER:

MY NOTES:

_____

_____

_____

_____

_____

HOW I FEEL ABOUT MY SAILING TODAY

A RECORD OF MY DAY:

DATE: _____

PLACE: _____

WEATHER:

MY NOTES:

_____
_____
_____
_____
_____

HOW I FEEL ABOUT MY SAILING TODAY

A RECORD OF MY DAY:

DATE: _____

PLACE: _____

WEATHER:

MY NOTES:

_____
_____
_____
_____
_____

HOW I FEEL ABOUT MY SAILING TODAY

A RECORD OF MY DAY:

DATE: _____

PLACE: _____

WEATHER:

MY NOTES:

_____
_____
_____
_____
_____

HOW I FEEL ABOUT MY SAILING TODAY

A RECORD OF MY DAY:

DATE: _____

PLACE: _____

WEATHER:

MY NOTES:

_____

_____

_____

_____

_____

HOW I FEEL ABOUT MY SAILING TODAY

A RECORD OF MY DAY:

DATE: _____

PLACE: _____

WEATHER:

MY NOTES:

_____

_____

_____

_____

_____

HOW I FEEL ABOUT MY SAILING TODAY

A RECORD OF MY DAY:

DATE: _____

PLACE: _____

WEATHER:

MY NOTES:

_____
_____
_____
_____
_____

HOW I FEEL ABOUT MY SAILING TODAY

A RECORD OF MY DAY:

DATE: _____

PLACE: _____

WEATHER:

MY NOTES:

_____

_____

_____

_____

_____

_____

HOW I FEEL ABOUT MY SAILING TODAY

A RECORD OF MY DAY:

DATE: _____

PLACE: _____

WEATHER:

MY NOTES:

_____

_____

_____

_____

_____

HOW I FEEL ABOUT MY SAILING TODAY

A RECORD OF MY DAY:

DATE: _____

PLACE: _____

WEATHER:

MY NOTES:

_____
_____
_____
_____
_____

HOW I FEEL ABOUT MY SAILING TODAY

A RECORD OF MY DAY:

```



```

DATE: _____

PLACE: _____

WEATHER:

MY NOTES:

_____

_____

_____

_____

_____

HOW I FEEL ABOUT MY SAILING TODAY

A RECORD OF MY DAY:

DATE: _____

PLACE: _____

WEATHER:

MY NOTES:

_____

_____

_____

_____

_____

HOW I FEEL ABOUT MY SAILING TODAY

A RECORD OF MY DAY:

DATE: _____

PLACE: _____

WEATHER:

MY NOTES:

_____

_____

_____

_____

_____

HOW I FEEL ABOUT MY SAILING TODAY

A RECORD OF MY DAY:

DATE: _____

PLACE: _____

WEATHER:

MY NOTES:

_____
_____
_____
_____
_____
_____

HOW I FEEL ABOUT MY SAILING TODAY

A RECORD OF MY DAY:

DATE: _____

PLACE: _____

WEATHER:

MY NOTES:

_____

_____

_____

_____

_____

HOW I FEEL ABOUT MY SAILING TODAY

A RECORD OF MY DAY:

DATE: _____

PLACE: _____

WEATHER:

MY NOTES:

_____

_____

_____

_____

_____

HOW I FEEL ABOUT MY SAILING TODAY

A RECORD OF MY DAY:

DATE: _____

PLACE: _____

WEATHER:

MY NOTES:

_____

_____

_____

_____

_____

HOW I FEEL ABOUT MY SAILING TODAY

A RECORD OF MY DAY:

DATE: _____

PLACE: _____

WEATHER:

MY NOTES:

_____
_____
_____
_____
_____

HOW I FEEL ABOUT MY SAILING TODAY

A RECORD OF MY DAY:

DATE: _____

PLACE: _____

WEATHER:

MY NOTES:

_____

_____

_____

_____

_____

HOW I FEEL ABOUT MY SAILING TODAY

A RECORD OF MY DAY:

DATE: _____

PLACE: _____

WEATHER:

MY NOTES:

_____
_____
_____
_____
_____

HOW I FEEL ABOUT MY SAILING TODAY

A RECORD OF MY DAY:

DATE: _____

PLACE: _____

WEATHER:

MY NOTES:

_____

_____

_____

_____

_____

HOW I FEEL ABOUT MY SAILING TODAY

A RECORD OF MY DAY:

DATE: _____

PLACE: _____

WEATHER:

MY NOTES:
_____
_____
_____
_____
_____

HOW I FEEL ABOUT MY SAILING TODAY

A RECORD OF MY DAY:

DATE: _____

PLACE: _____

WEATHER:

MY NOTES:

_____

_____

_____

_____

_____

HOW I FEEL ABOUT MY SAILING TODAY

A RECORD OF MY DAY:

DATE: _____

PLACE: _____

WEATHER:

MY NOTES:

_____

_____

_____

_____

_____

HOW I FEEL ABOUT MY SAILING TODAY

A RECORD OF MY DAY:

DATE: _____

PLACE: _____

WEATHER:

MY NOTES:

_____

_____

_____

_____

_____

HOW I FEEL ABOUT MY SAILING TODAY

A RECORD OF MY DAY:

DATE: _____

PLACE: _____

WEATHER:

MY NOTES:

_____

_____

_____

_____

_____

_____

HOW I FEEL ABOUT MY SAILING TODAY

A RECORD OF MY DAY:

DATE: _____

PLACE: _____

WEATHER:

MY NOTES:

_____
_____
_____
_____
_____

HOW I FEEL ABOUT MY SAILING TODAY

A RECORD OF MY DAY:

DATE: _____

PLACE: _____

WEATHER:

MY NOTES:

_____

_____

_____

_____

_____

HOW I FEEL ABOUT MY SAILING TODAY

A RECORD OF MY DAY:

DATE: _____

PLACE: _____

WEATHER:

MY NOTES:

_____

_____

_____

_____

_____

HOW I FEEL ABOUT MY SAILING TODAY

A RECORD OF MY DAY:

DATE: _____

PLACE: _____

WEATHER:

MY NOTES:

_____
_____
_____
_____
_____

HOW I FEEL ABOUT MY SAILING TODAY

A RECORD OF MY DAY:

DATE: _____

PLACE: _____

WEATHER:

MY NOTES:

_____

_____

_____

_____

_____

HOW I FEEL ABOUT MY SAILING TODAY

A RECORD OF MY DAY:

.

Printed in Great Britain
by Amazon